Whispers of a time.

A dedicated collection of poetry.

Written by: Mr. Stephen G. Wright

Copyright © 2022 by Stephen G. Wright

All rights reserved. No part of this book may be reproduced or transmitted in any form or by any means, electronic or mechanical, including photocopying, recording, or any information storage and retrieval system, without permission in writing from the author.

ISBN: 978-0-9986462-3-7 - Paperback

∞This paper meets the requirements of ANSI/NISO Z39.48-1992 (Permanence of Paper)

Cover photo
By Mr. Eric Muhr
online at: ericmuhr.photo

The author wishes to Thank Mr. Muhr for his kind permission (April, 2022) to utilize his photograph for this book.

This collection is dedicated to

my maternal Grandmother

Mary Brett Byrne

During my childhood "Nana" would read to me the vast array of poems she had written. Friends of hers always encouraged her to publish as her skill in poetry was excellent. Regrettably, sadly, she never did. It is my deepest pain that all her poems appear to have been lost. It is more than a pity to have known such a talent and to have not been able to share that with you. It is faint tribute to offer my simpler, yet similar, prose as an attempt at recompense for having not safeguarded her legacy better.

Eulogy in Thanks

I sat in quiet reflection
before picking up my pen.
There was so much to think of,
the words I'd heard back then.

Those words did not always find me,
often, passing by my ears.
Strangely the words stayed with me
through the passing of the years.

The passage of time gave meaning
to the poems of long ago.
Words of joy or comfort,
perhaps to help us grow.

The miracle of imagination
could be found in every rhyme,
Playful flights of fancy,
diminished not by time.

Leprechauns, goblins and snowmen,
seemed eternal in her fairyland.
And spoke she of a golden key,
to a castle made of sand.

Far more than simple fantasy
lay hidden within the pages.
So very few of us read with insight
to the wisdom of the ages.

In childhood the words were hollow,
but they echoed in my mind,
reminding me of some message,
a lasting lesson of a kind.

I did not always know her purpose,
but in my soul, she left a seed,
Now I pass the same on to yours,
somehow, you must believe!

In Simple Terms

If one phrase tells what life is about,
    It is that life is unfair.
If one-word states what life should be,
    It is then to care.

But life is often not so simple,
    as a phrase or poignant word.
Perhaps it is best understood,
    if every voice is heard.

See those around you as equals,
    for they may look to you.
Perhaps they seek a kind word,
    or a helping hand or two.

Seek out truth in all endeavors,
teach others of what you find.
All is gained to your soul,
for but once being kind.

No word, no phrase, no poetry,
can set your life's course,
but maybe, oh but maybe now,
you'll face life without remorse

6/24/78 @ 1:43am

In Challenge to a Hypocrite

I'll not tender any thoughts from thee

that border on hypocrisy!

Nor shall I allow a wretched bore

to waste away my time much more.

For of your rhyme and reason,

I have had my fill,

and fancy I, in such constraint,

feel all the better still.

I keep my words straight and true,

and challenge thee not to misconstrue.

So, hold your tongue again I say

whilst I strip your mask away!

Time

Without regulation of time or restriction of space,
   to be all alone in an empty place –
allows a man's mind to stop and ponder,
   it allows a man's mind to quietly wander.

Some find time and it's meaning a bother,
   some worship time as a Father.
Some run their lives by the clock on the wall,
   while others live without worry at all.

I do not see time as my lord.
   With increasing talk of time – I'm bored!
Time to me is a relative thing.
   I'll always wonder what time will bring.

A Book

Today I took a book in hand,
   with passing pages, trying to understand,
why I felt a growing sense of fear,
   about her picture drawing near.

My curiosity continued to burn,
   so, on I went, each page in turn.
'Til then and there I reached the place,
   upon which I gazed down at her face.

I turned the page and then another,
   'til again I saw that long-lost lover!
Why prolong this pain? What is it for?
   So, I closed that book forever more.

A Little Christmas Toast

With this holiday upon us,

we think of those for whom we care most.

With this in mind, I felt compelled

to write this little Christmas toast:

May you and yours always have

   the best in every way.

May your joy in living be,

   multiplied day by day.

May you find in those around you

   the strength to meet life's trials.

May your journeys be blessed with safety,

   regardless of the miles.

So, from this humble poet,

to all those far and near —

I wish a very Merry Christmas

and a prosperous New Year!

Christmas of '77

Let us reflect on what Christmas should mean.
Let us believe in what cannot be seen.
Let us thank God for each of our friends.
Let us remember our existence on God depends.

But let us also remember Christ's birth
and the reasons he was here on Earth.
As war, hatred, and hunger seem never to cease,
Jesus always said, the answer is peace!

The Sound

All the trees have lost their leaves.

Snow has fallen to the ground.

The streets are alive with grand excitement.

Each person hopes to hear the sound.

Homes are brightened with decoration.

Brothers and sisters are homeward bound.

Thoughts drift back to childhood,

simple times – filled with the sound.

Good will seems to prevail in us all.

We try to help the lost be found.

Give a dollar for the poor,

did you hear the sound?

Friends and family, rich and poor,

join hands and gather round.

Smile now at one another,

I hope we'll hear the sound!

Bow down your heads one and all.

Let all your questions cease.

Now has come the appointed time,

to hear the sound of peace.

I am my father's son.

Do you think as we grow
   we think only of our life's run?
Do you believe I have forgotten,
   I am my father's son?

Please take a moment and ponder
   upon the things we say and do.
Think of yourself while growing up,
   are we not then much like you?

I know at times you wonder,
   if we have any sense at all.
We must learn from each day we live,
   from the many times we fall.

Bound by the past and lineage

   we face life's insincerity.

We've gained from our father

   a sense of honor and integrity.

Worry not for our future,

   have faith in what you have done.

My brothers and I are proud to say,

   we are our father's sons.

Stephen G.

Some people seem to think I am

a borderline neurotic.

Some people seem to think I am

a borderline psychotic.

Yet I wonder why they worry.

I ponder why they care.

For I am just a helpless, hapless nut –

who is neither here nor there!

Insight

There is music in your laughter,

warmth within your heart.

There is a sparkle in your eyes

when a smile you impart.

Others may not see as I

the beauty I admire.

But I have felt your gentleness,

and the hope that you inspire.

Perfume

A sweet smell triggers my memory.

I find my thoughts in a velvet cloud.

For a fleeting moment I feel that memory,

with that pain – I cry aloud.

Her ghost, I swear, haunts this day.

Her heart no tear will shed.

I am the victim of my imagination,

it's only the smell of perfume in my head.

The Bar – '81

All that I am, I offer.
   Yet to whom and why, I ask?
Trying so hard not to be alone
   is such a lonely task.
Sitting but a few inches away,
   exchanging words and a smile.
I feel that I should say much more,
   in such a very short while.
But like the many times before,
   I lack their social grace.
And find I'm sitting quite alone,
   in a not so lonely place.

A Passing Thought.

Here I sit, all alone,

in my little humble home,

passing the minutes, worrying away,

trying to think of things to say.

If things were only simpler,

and my worries a little littler,

I'm sure that I would quickly find,

I could, just once, make up my mind!

To my friends – 10/09/78.

What can I say to you,

  those that who care enough,

to make this birthday the happiest

  when times seem a little rough.

How is it God so blesses me,

  that you each might be here now?

You've made my life much fuller,

  despite the wrinkles in my brow.

For you have, on this day, made clear

  how much our life depends

on people who are good and kind;

  proudly I call friends!

Stark Reality

Nights drew long with thoughts of you.

A dazzling haze of emotion.

A morning sun, a silent one,

a victim of self-demotion?

Woman of self-made innocence,

see beauty in simplicity.

Far and near, harsh and dear.

A shared problem of complicity.

Shyness perhaps a mortal curse.

Defenses in clouded reason.

A dream fulfilled? Hopes are killed!

Still welcome with each passing season.

Seasons of the Heart

I once walked with summer's rain,

but now I walk with winter's pain.

I once rejoiced in Spring and Fall,

but now I feel no joy at all.

I once felt the sun's warming rays,

but now I feel only cold, dark days.

The joys of life in my mind are planted,

I find now, I took them all for granted.

Where once was body, there is only bone.

For now, again, I am alone.

A Poem for the Family Vineyard

Consider a flooded vineyard my friends -
pity the picker's awful plight.
Picking grapes in waste high water
surely is not right.

Yet see such determination,
as he strains to pick the crop.
Would you care to wager that he says,
this madness has to stop?

So, your family has a vineyard,
your hands turn purple as you pick.
Indeed, when first I saw your hands,
I fancied you were sick.

Grape picking is not my worry,
   and certainly not my wish.
My only concern for grapes my friend
   is if they are in bottle or in dish.

Some like grapes for eating,
   others prefer wine, like me.
So that is why I say, get back to work.
   I'm running low you see!

A Good Light Tonight

There is a good light tonight.
    It shines upon me now
It fills the cavern in my soul,
    and soothes my doubts, somehow.
It lifts me to far reaching heights,
    and removes my great despair.
It moves my heart to passion,
    and allows my heart to care.
Know that as I've changed and grown,
    I may have seen great strife.
There is a good light tonight.
    You are that light – you are my life!

In Perspective

I, in fact, have had my day
   when I could choose the games I play.
Now I see I played it wrong.
   I played with fire far too long.
As each day goes by, I seem better off,
   for the experience of one love lost.
Better to wait till youth grows old,
   for then you're smarter, not so bold.
I feel no guilt over the path I've taken.
   I simply see that I was mistaken.
I let my life run its course,
   saddened, yes but without remorse.
When all is really said and done -
   you've had your laughs, and had your fun,
You begin to see how foolish you've been,
   wishing you'd been more wise back then!

Whosoever Will

Who will sing a song for me,

when I'm feeling down?

Who will wear a smile for me,

when all I do is frown?

Who will walk a mile with me,

when I walk alone?

Who will come and warm me,

when I shiver to the bone?

Who will guide me through hard times,

when I am too blind to see?

All these things I will do for you –

if you will do the same for me.

Where I Once Walked

I see the young growing old,
   as they walk where I once walked.
They are growing up, or so I'm told,
   as they talk how I once talked.

I see them every now and then,
   as they play games I once played.
Yet when I start remembering when,
   I've stayed where I shouldn't have stayed.

With going back I'm filled with woe.
     For time goes on and children grow,
         into adults I don't quite know.

Mind's Tide

As the hands of every clock move by,
   or comes the night at end of day,
So to do our memories go,
   as the mind's tide slips away.
The tide rolls in to swell our thoughts,
   yet comes with it an undertow.
All too soon it pulls away,
   the cherished things we know.
Oh, damn the march of time!
   It is the tide's only friend.
They work to diminish us,
   and all the sweet memories we depend.

Awaiting Love

Oh, but love, enticing fold,
   embrace me once lest I grow old.
All good patience will surely ebb,
   when left counting stars far overhead.

So long I've sought your warmth and grace.
   For my heart is a cold and empty place.
How is it that you tease me so?
   You play me a fool then swiftly go.

Stay, I plead, but for a while,
   and end for me this lonely trial.
But no, you elude me once again,
   usurp my feelings disguised as friend.

You dart about in rodent fashion,

    a hardened killer devoid of passion.

Curse, oh curse, this mortal love,

    and pray deliverance from above.

Perhaps it is that I am a fool,

    used and discarded as some ancient tool.

But for all the melancholy days,

    that I have spent in sorrowful ways –

I find I am still drawn near

    to the promise of love - oh so dear!

Of Mysteries Deep Within

Pray, do my eyes deceive me,
    to what may lie within?
Sweet angelic wisdom,
    or the complicity of sin?!
A woman's heart is closely guarded,
    so each man may misconstrue –
the actions that they ponder
    and may subsequently do!

Retrospect

It was but for a moment,
    that I remembered days long past.
It brought to mind too many things,
    that traveled by so fast.
It was in winter we grew together,
    and in the winter our demise.
Yet after so many years,
    now a different feeling I did surmise.
For with all bitterness aside,
    and hostilities at an end,
when now I look, I see no long-lost love,
    I see at last two friends.
I have such bittersweet memories,
    but they all seem but a haze,
for they like many other things,
    were in my younger days.

For Moments Gone

Silence seems a stronger voice,

it fosters doubt but little choice.

Questions racing through my mind –

convenient answers seem unkind.

Each moment that I spent with you,

seemed to paint the world anew.

Laughter sprang up with simple grace.

I adored the radiance in your face.

Yet, I always felt your thoughts divided,

and feared the cost if they collided.

Your heart was always kind, tis true,

to give it seemed to frighten you.

How brave the need that you be fair,

for another you should despair.

Does he deserve a heart so true?

What in him so inspires you?

Perhaps I do not inspire passion,

for I pipe after a different fashion.

Regardless of who be right or wrong,

faint reward are moments gone!

Face the Wind

Ill fate, where is thy victory,
   that I should face the morrow cold?
Grant a pleasant memory,
   then strike thy dagger bold!

To Doubt the Day

      My presence is but a fleeting thing,
         it's worth grows less with age.
      Seeming with each passing day,
         I'm just a well-read page!

Timely Age and Wisdom

Tis true, with age comes wisdom.
   For I have suffered not.
I've found patience and propriety,
   from me most ungainly lot.
So, let the days come passing,
   as the years reflect an age.
We are all great books of knowledge,
   adding to thee, page by page!

A Dream to Curse the Day

My mood was somber, my mood was surly,
   for the dawn was breaking – far too early!
I much preferred the land of dreams,
   with its inventive, convoluted schemes.
Darkened paths and moonlight skies,
   thoughts of dispersion and demise.
Existence here is of my creation,
   standing ground against damnation!
The future is, as I may cast.
   I dismiss, off hand, ghosts of my past.
Yet always comes the time to awaken;
   time when self-important dreams are shaken.
With dreams of power – dreams of wealth,
   the greatest enemy is yourself!
Dreams breed hope and give me pause.
   Dreams allow me to win a hopeless cause.
Dreams seem best in the dark of night –
   best they be tempered by dawns light.

Past Midnight

While you have slept, I sat waiting,
  curious to see dawns breaking.
Are such times meant for (quiet) repose?
  Or for quaint, vicarious prose?
The wee hours are not loud or bright.
  The world an eerie peace this night.
A furry friend did just scamper through.
  Odd company for me to keep, tis true!
With such time to spare as this,
  humans offer scant little bliss.
Ask ye, who am I to raise a fuss,
  'bout things that most would not discuss?
For while I've pondered questions deep –
  You've gained little more than sleep!

In the Face of Disillusionment

Why are you silent?

People laugh at what I say!

Why are you angry?

No one seems to care today!

Why are you afraid?

People kill without regard!

Why are you untrusting?

Safer is the heart that is hard!

Why do you not listen?

All that I hear is slanted!

Why are you selfish?

My kindness is taken for granted!

Why are you alone?

Others have no time for me!

Why are you bitter?

Humans look but never see!

Why are you alive? --- I have faith!!

The Calling

Do not feel sad for me
as my hour comes anon.
Tis a voice, oh but a whisper,
bids now I travel on.
Do not strain to hear it.
It doth beckon only I.
Resolved, I am, to face the dark,
alone as day draws neigh.
Be glad! Your love goes with me,
for the journey on ahead.
Seek the calling in your heart –
pay heed to what I've said!

The Bird of Gentle Beauty

How rare is this bird that greets me.
   How sweet is the song you sing.
No trial of life defeats me,
   as I see you taking wing.

You've brought out the richness of living.
   You inspire joy each day.
Your heart is kind – your heart is giving,
   yet you may soon take all of this away.

Sometimes your eyes are sparkling, bright,
   sometimes brooding, scared and sad.
Things are dealt with, taken far from sight.
   Our lives are created, not may have had.

How rare this bird that touches my soul.
   A gentle spirit touched me from the start.
Share life's joy with me, as I seek one goal,
   To show, I'm worthy of your heart.

Soar sweet bird – soar high.
   Don't be afraid to touch the sky.
Dearest one soon return here,
   each day I long to have you near.

Food for Thought

(with thanks to Elizabeth Barret Browning!)

"How do I love thee –

let me count the ways."

I love you like a banana split

or a luscious orange duck glaze.

I love you like a pork chop,

I love you like a steak.

I wish you were a leg of lamb

that I could marinate.

I love you like a Hershey bar,

I love you like a sunday.

I wish you were a Snickers,

I could munch on every Monday.

I love you like a burger,

I love you like a ham.

I wish you were some sauerkraut,

Smothered all in Spam.

You are my little sausage,

You are my pot of Irish stew.

Isn't clear to you by now,

I want to sublimate you!!!

Will thou Remember?

Whence came the great turn of time,

the light of future did grow nigh.

Think back on stories told you,

as I relive those days gone by.

Did not a spirit embrace us all,

for too short a thousand days?

All too soon the spirit died,

to insure the older ways.

The ways were not of brotherhood,

for fear of what it brought.

Coexistence, they preferred it not be taught!

Fear not my friends,

some faithful still remained.

Philosophies of peace and truth

were guarded and retained.

But the veneer of youth tranquility

would not for too long last,

storm clouds were on the horizon,

and signaled trouble coming fast.

Lightening flashed out in the West,

and it came with roles of thunder.

The storm arrived with furry,

to tear the land asunder.

Leaders are being killed in the streets.

There was a bomb's shattering blast.

The time had come to stand our ground,

the youth rebellion came at last!

The night was filled with fire,

Mothers held their children near.

Let everyone know our furry,

as the end has come, I fear!

Yet, cities did not fall to ruin,

nor did streets crumble from marching feet.

We did not hear the trumpet sound,

to call for our retreat.

Whence came the great turn of time,

we moved again toward status quo.

Those whom we fought had remained,

the counterculture had to go!

I say not that we have lost,

nor say I others won.

I say only we survive,

and survive we must – as one.

So, this question now I pose to you,

lest this decade breed regret –

for principle will thou remember,

or from ignorance, will thou forget?

If Just by Questions Asked

Pray tell me then, what will become of me,
   if not this life of mediocrity?
What is it that should be my gain,
   if in this world I shall remain?

Will I find love or just remorse,
   by staying to this mortal course?
My patience now seems but a thread,
   as my days are filled with dread.

A constant feeling of rejection,
   is cause enough for introspection!
Do questions of life and death reveal,
   the answers our emotions conceal?

My feelings may sound as a battle joined,

    phrases that some ancient writer coined.

These feelings mare my soul like rust,

    but with time fade and blow away as dust.

What will I have won by embracing night,

    and giving up this righteous fight?

I may question faith, yet wait till dawn,

    to seek again answers to which I'm drawn.

Save Tomorrow for Tomorrow

If we, for only a moment saw,
   all the days that lay ahead,
we would have no further reason
   to live with futures dread.

With the coming of each morning,
   we would rise with great assurance.
For the knowledge of the future,
   is an undeniable insurance.

Dear friends it was never meant for us
   to see our course in life.
It was ordained that we should
   overcome our troubles, fear and strife.

It is our test to face each year
   with tolerance and reason,
To have each passing day and week,
   a reflection of each season.

If we, for only a moment see,
   all our days, life's mysteries bare,
We'd choose the peace we find in faith,
   and the simple comfort of a prayer!

"Remember man..."

Was it you who gave the moon it's glow?
Was it you who brought the winter snow?
Was it you who made clouds fill the sky?
Was it you who taught the birds to fly?

Can you create the elk or deer?
Can you make the rain appear?
Can you call upon the winds great force?
Can you change a typhoons course?

Was it you who gave us night and day,
and gave each season it's proper stay?
Was it you who gave the oceans depth,
defined the deserts length and breadth?

You are like grains of sand in space –
grains of sand that carve a mountains face!

Other Books by Stephen G. Wright

Reasoned Globality, New Organizational Pathways for International Professionals.

This book was created based on research, observations, and interactions with professionals in the U.S. and abroad. The book seeks to redefine the perceptions we hold of human interactions and relationships within organizations and beyond.

Eminent Reckoning.

This rather unique review of the topic of diversity is based on university guest lectures given since 2021. The book endeavors to open a new and different approach to how we, as people in the States, define ourselves. Maintaining an open mind to new perceptions and possibilities would be advised when reading Eminent Reckoning!

Contact Mr. Wright

Email: proftype@live.com
Web Site: www.reasonedglobality.com

www.ingramcontent.com/pod-product-compliance
Lightning Source LLC
Chambersburg PA
CBHW010449010526
44118CB00019B/2521